◇TELL ME ABOUT◇

PEOPLE & PLACES

SERIES EDITOR: JACKIE GAFF

ILLUSTRATED BY CHRIS FORSEY

Kingfisher Books

Series editor: Jackie Gaff
Series designer: Terry Woodley
Author: Moira Butterfield
Contributor: Angela Royston
Designer: David West Children's Book Design
Illustrators: Chris Forsey (pp 2–31, 38);
Kevin Madison (pp. 32–33, 36–37);
Valerie Sangster (pp. 34–35)
Cover illustration: Chris Forsey
Editor: Mike Halson

Kingfisher Books, Grisewood & Dempsey Ltd,
Elsley House, 24–30 Great Titchfield Street,
London W1P 7AD

First published in 1991 by Kingfisher Books
Copyright © Grisewood & Dempsey Ltd 1991

BRITISH LIBRARY CATALOGUING IN PUBLICATION DATA
People and places.
  1. Social life
  I. Gaff, Jackie   II. Forsey, Chris   III. Series
  909.829

ISBN 0 86272 564 X
Phototypeset by Southern Positives and Negatives
(SPAN), Lingfield, Surrey.
Printed in Spain.

Contents

How many people are there?   4

What is a country?   6

Which is the world's biggest
  country?   8

Which is the world's smallest
  country?   8

Which is the most visited country?   9

How many languages are there?   10

Which language do most people
  speak?   11

What is a government?   12

What is a parliament?   13

What are taxes?   13

Which are the main religions?   14

What is Mardi Gras?   16

When is Chinese New Year?   17

Who was Santa Claus?   17

Why do we wear different clothes? 18

When were the first theatres built? 20

Why do we play music? 21

When did painting begin? 21

Which is the oldest sport? 22

When were the first Olympic Games? 22

Which is the most popular sport? 23

How many different jobs are there? 24

What is the most popular food? 26

Who eats the most food? 26

Where are the biggest farms? 27

Do all children go to school? 28

What is the School of the Air? 29

Why do some schools have uniforms? 29

What are minerals? 30

Which are the main fuels? 31

Why are houses so different? 32

How do people live in the Sahara Desert? 34

How do people live in the Arctic? 34

How do people live in the Himalayas? 35

How do people live in the Amazon? 35

What is a city? 36

How will we live in the future? 38

Useful words 39

Index 40

How many people are there?

There are about 5 billion people living in the world today. The number of people who live in a particular place or area is known as its population. For thousands of years the world's population increased slowly. But over the past 200 years there has been a population explosion and the number of people living in the world has increased dramatically. If this continues, there will be nearly three times as many people in 60 years' time!

POPULATION FACTS

● Over 200,000 people are born every day – that's about 140 babies a minute!

● Currently, one person in three is under the age of 15.

● The country with the biggest population is China. About 1 billion people live there – one fifth of the world's population.

● Japanese people tend to live longest. On average, they live for nearly 75 years.

1 In 8000 BC there were about 6 million people in the world. At that time, most people lived in the continents of Asia and Africa.

DO YOU KNOW

Human beings have only been around for a tiny fraction of the Earth's existence.
   Imagine that the Earth was formed exactly one year ago – on 1 January. That would mean that our earliest ancestors did not appear until the afternoon of 31 December!

2 By AD 1, the world's population had grown to about 255 million people. People now lived in most parts of the world.

5 By 2050, there may be as many as 14 billion people in the world – nearly three times as many as there are today!

4 In the 1900s, the population has shot up to 5 billion. That's over ten times as many people as there were in 1500.

DO YOU KNOW

We use the letters BC and AD to show that we are counting years from the birth of Jesus Christ. BC means Before Christ, and AD stands for *Anno Domini*, which is Latin for 'Year of our Lord'.

Remember that BC dates count backwards – so 1000 BC is a more recent date than 2000 BC.

3 In 1500 the population had nearly doubled, to about 460 million people – about half the population of India today.

Birth of Christ

BC			AD
2000	1000	0	2000

◄──── 4000 years ────►

What is a country?

A country is an area of land which is independent – its people control all their own affairs. The country has a boundary and a name which are recognized by other countries. It also has its own flag and a national anthem, or song.

There are about 170 countries in the world at present, but the number keeps changing as new countries are created, or two countries join together.

KEY TO MAP

1	Albania	34	Haiti	65	San Marino
2	Andorra	35	Honduras	66	Senegal
3	Austria	36	Hungary	67	Sierra Leone
4	Bahrain	37	Iceland	68	Singapore
5	Bangladesh	38	Ireland	69	Sri Lanka
6	Belgium	39	Jamaica	70	Surinam
7	Belize	40	Jordan	71	Swaziland
8	Benin	41	Kampuchea (Cambodia)	72	Switzerland
9	Bhutan			73	Taiwan
10	Brunei	42	Korea, North	74	Thailand
11	Bulgaria	43	Korea, South	75	Togo
12	Burkina Faso	44	Kuwait	76	Trinidad and Tobago
13	Burundi	45	Lesotho		
14	Central African Republic	46	Liberia	77	Tunisia
		47	Liechtenstein	78	United Arab Emirates
15	Costa Rica	48	Luxembourg		
16	Cuba	49	Malawi	79	Uruguay
17	Cyprus	50	Malta	80	Vatican City
18	Czechoslovakia	51	Monaco	81	Vietnam
19	Denmark	52	Netherlands	82	Yugoslavia
20	Djibouti	53	New Zealand	83	Zimbabwe
21	Dominica	54	Nicaragua		
22	Dominican Republic	55	Panama		
23	Ecuador	56	Papua New Guinea		
24	El Salvador	57	Philippines		
25	Equatorial Guinea	58	Portugal		
26	Gambia	59	Qatar		
27	Germany	60	Romania		
28	Ghana	61	Rwanda		
29	Great Britain	62	St Christopher and Nevis		
30	Greece				
31	Guatemala	63	St Lucia		
32	Guinea-Bissau	64	St Vincent and the Grenadines		
33	Guyana				

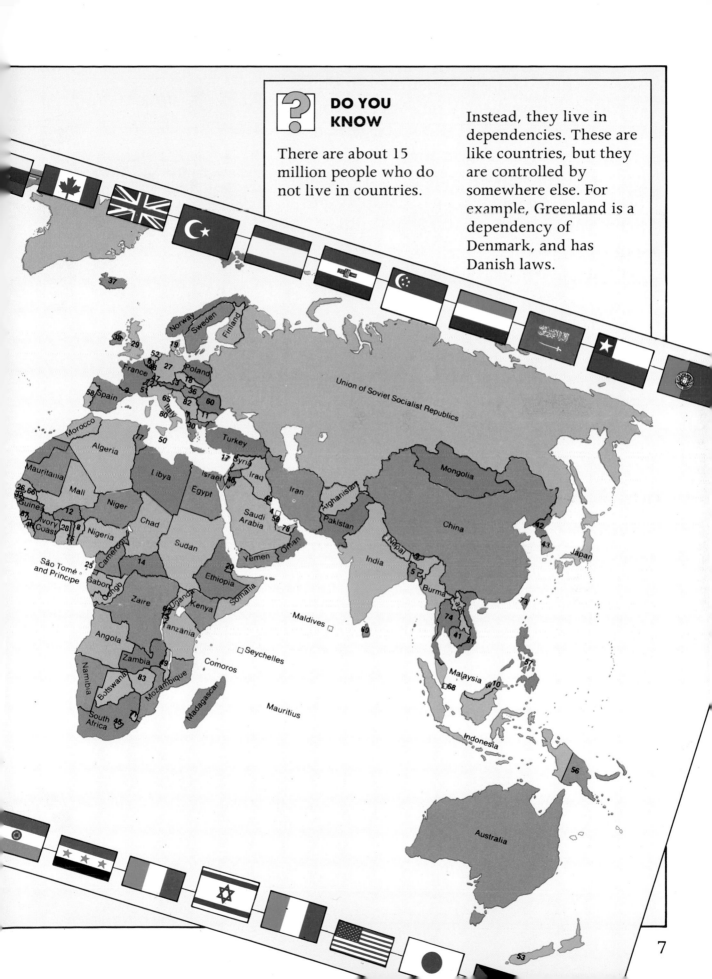

DO YOU KNOW

There are about 15 million people who do not live in countries.

Instead, they live in dependencies. These are like countries, but they are controlled by somewhere else. For example, Greenland is a dependency of Denmark, and has Danish laws.

37

Norway

Sweden

Finland

36

29

52

19

8

27

France

Poland

18

47

33

36

58 Spain

9

65

82

60

51

80

Italy

11

Morocco

30

77

50

Turkey

Algeria

17 Syria

Mauritania

Libya

Israel

46

Iraq

26 66

Mali

Egypt

Iran

Afghanistan

Niger

44

Guinea

12

Saudi

Arabia

4 58

78

Ivory

28

8

Nigeria

Pakistan

China

42

Coast

15

Chad

Oman

43

Japan

Cameroon

Sudan

Nepal

India

São Tomé

and Principe

25

Gabon

Yemen

20

3

Congo

14

Ethiopia

Burma

5

Zaire

Uganda

Kenya

Somalia

Maldives

69

73

Tanzania

74

Angola

Seychelles

41

81

Zambia

89

Comoros

57

Namibia

83

Mozambique

Malaysia

10

Botswana

Madagascar

68

South

45

Mauritius

Africa

Indonesia

56

Australia

Union of Soviet Socialist Republics

Mongolia

53

7

Which is the world's biggest country?

The USSR is the biggest country in the world. It covers nearly one-seventh of the Earth's land area, and it is so large that when it is night-time in some parts of the country, other parts are still in daylight! Because of its size, this vast country has many different kinds of climate and countryside.

USSR FACTS

● It would take over two years to walk round the borders of the USSR – a journey of 106,000 km.

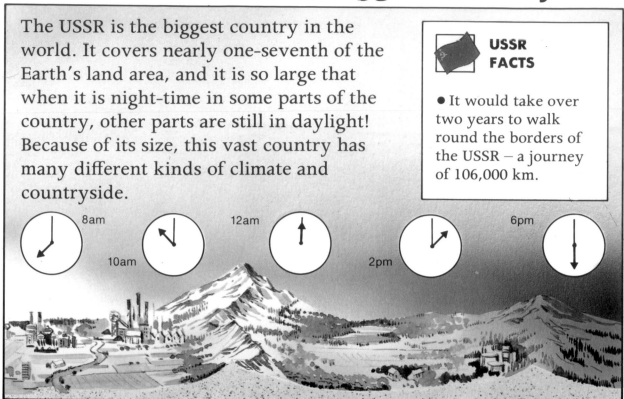

Which is the world's smallest country?

The smallest independent country is the State of the Vatican City in the Italian city of Rome. It covers an area of 44 hectares – about the size of an average city park. It is the headquarters of the Roman Catholic Church and has a tiny population of just 1000 people.

? DO YOU KNOW

The Vatican City has its own flag, radio station and railway It even issues its own stamps!

8

Which is the most visited country?

The country with the highest number of visitors is Spain, which has about 42 million tourists every year. It is followed by France, then the USA, Italy, Austria, the UK and Canada. The number of tourists is growing fast, as more and more people decide to go abroad for their holidays.

 DO YOU KNOW

When visiting another country, you usually have to show your passport. This is a document which says who you are, what you look like and which country you are from. The word passport comes from documents used for ships visiting ports.

The most popular tourist spots in Spain are the magnificent beaches along its Mediterranean coast.

France is the second-most visited country. Its most famous sight is the spectacular Eiffel Tower in Paris.

The USA has 23 million visitors a year. The Statue of Liberty, in New York Harbor, is a popular attraction.

Italy is visited by 20 million people a year. The Colosseum in Rome is one of the world's best-known tourist spots.

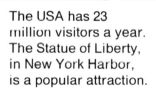 **MAKE A POSTER**

Find out more about your area by making a big tourist poster. List some interesting sites to visit and things to do. Add some photos, postcards or pictures cut from magazines to show the places that you think tourists should visit.

Unlike a lot of other tourist countries, Austria is busiest in the winter, during the skiing season.

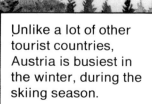

How many languages are there?

Nearly 5000 languages are spoken around the world, but many are only used by small groups of people. In India, for example, there are 16 main languages, but around 1000 minor ones which are only spoken in certain parts of the country.

These children are all saying 'hello'. The words are written down as they sound, rather than as they're spelt.

The Sun is in the sky.

The master is in the house.

JAM-BO

Swahili is spoken all along the east coast of Africa.

MAR-HU-BA

Many forms of Arabic are spoken throughout the Middle East.

KON-NEE-CHEE-WA

Japanese is spoken by the 124 million people of Japan.

The first written languages used picture symbols instead of an alphabet made up of different letters. One of the earliest symbol languages was developed in Egypt about 5000 years ago. These ancient symbols are called hieroglyphs.

Two simple hieroglyphic sentences are shown above.

BWEN-OS DEE-OS

Spanish is spoken in Spain and most of South America.

NAM-AS-TAY

Hindi is spoken by about a third of the people in India.

ESPAÑA

10

Which language do most people speak?

The language with the largest number of speakers is Mandarin. It's the main language of China and it's spoken by over 715 million people.

Unlike English, Mandarin has no alphabet. Instead, it uses about 50,000 picture symbols called characters. Some words are formed by simple characters which are quite easy to understand. Other words are made up of two or more characters mixed together. One of the most complicated words is 'talkative' – it contains 64 characters!

 DO YOU KNOW

Pilots of every nationality use English to identify themselves when landing or taking off from any airport.

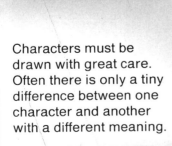

MAN   SKY

Characters must be drawn with great care. Often there is only a tiny difference between one character and another with a different meaning.

What is a government?

A government is a group of people who run a country – govern means run or rule. Governments are responsible for all sorts of things, from making new laws to collecting taxes and deciding how they should be spent. People involved in running the country are called politicians and the work they do is known as politics.

The members of the government with the most important jobs are sometimes called the cabinet.

In most countries, one person is chosen to head the government – as prime minister or president, for example.

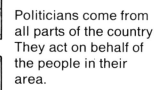

Politicians come from all parts of the country They act on behalf of the people in their area.

 GOVERNMENT FACTS

● In many countries, the people vote to elect, or choose, their government. This system is called a democracy. Voting takes place every few years, in general elections.

● A country headed by a king or queen is called a monarchy.

The Roman Emperor Julius Caesar was a dictator.

● Some countries are ruled by one person called a dictator.

● Communist countries are ruled by one very powerful group of politicians called the Communist Party.

What is a parliament?

A parliament is a body of people responsible for making a country's laws. One of the oldest parliaments is in the United Kingdom. It is made up of two houses, or parts. One house is for elected politicians, and the other is for nobles and churchmen.

The UK parliament meets in the Houses of Parliament on the bank of the River Thames in London. The famous old clock below is called Big Ben.

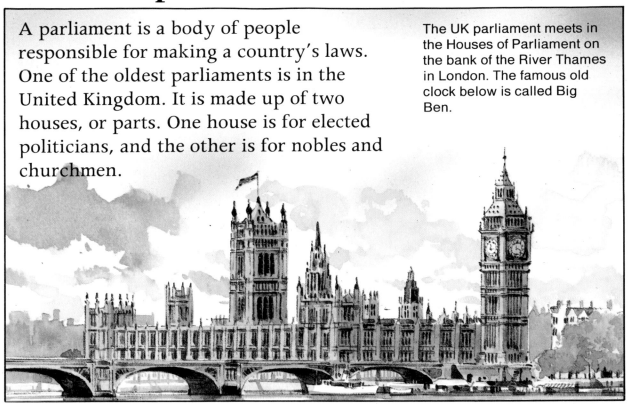

What are taxes?

Taxes are sums of money collected by governments from the people. They are needed to pay for services we all use, such as the police, the armed forces, education and health care.

Many countries have a free national health service, which anybody can use. This is paid for with money raised in taxes.

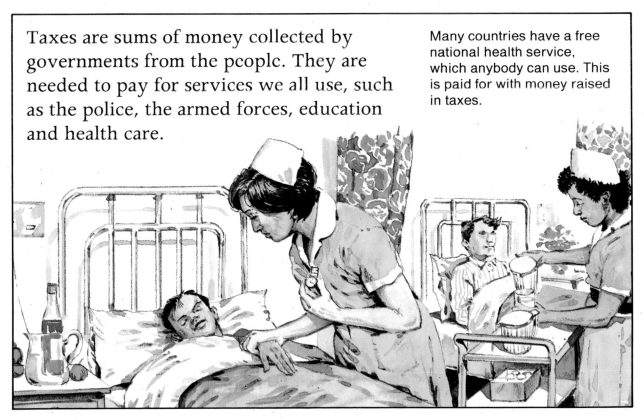

Which are the main religions?

The three largest religions in the world are Christianity, Islam and Hinduism. But there are also several other major religions, and thousands of smaller ones.

Each religion has its own beliefs and methods of worship. Some people believe there is just one god, while others believe there are many. Most religions have special ceremonies which are performed in holy buildings called temples or churches.

DO YOU KNOW

Evidence found inside caves shows that belief in gods goes back thousands of years. Ancient cave people used to perform dances and kill animals especially to please the gods and to get help from them.

Christianity was started nearly 2000 years ago by the followers of Jesus Christ. Christians believe in one god and in the teachings of a book called the Bible.

Hinduism is the main religion of India and other countries nearby. Its followers believe in many gods, but the most important ones are Brahma, Vishnu and Shiva.

● Followers of the Indian religion Jainism try never to harm any living creature.

● Christianity is followed by about a third of the world's population. Islam has the next biggest, with about a fifth of the world's population.

● The largest temple ever built is Angkor Wat (City Temple) in Kampuchea (Cambodia). It would take five hours to walk from one end to the other.

The followers of Judaism are called Jews. The religion was founded by Abraham in about 1900 BC. Jews believe in one god, and their holy book is the Hebrew Bible.

Islam was founded in Arabia by Muhammad in AD 622. Followers of the religion are called Muslims. They believe that there is one god, and their holy book is the Koran.

Buddhism is based on the teachings of Siddharta Gautama, an Indian prince who lived over 2500 years ago. Great teachers of this religion are given the title 'Buddha'.

What is Mardi Gras?

Mardi Gras is a festival that takes place in many countries every year on Shrove Tuesday. This is the last day before the time of year known as Lent, when Christians traditionally fast, or go without fat and meat. Mardi Gras is French for 'fat Tuesday'

During Mardi Gras, crowds of people wearing fancy dress parade through the streets and dance to the music of marching bands.

FESTIVAL FACTS

• The word festival means 'feast day'

• The Romans spent over 100 days a year feasting in honour of their gods.

• Dozens of countries round the world hold festivals on their Independence Day – to celebrate the time when they gained their freedom from foreign control.

MAKE A CARNIVAL MASK

Here's a way to make a carnival mask from card and wool.

1 Cut an oval shape out of thin card. Make holes for the eyes and mouth.

2 Paint on a face using brightly coloured pens. Stick coloured wool or paper strips around the top, to make hair.

3 Make a hole in each side of the mask, then thread a piece of wool through each hole and fix it with a knot.

When is Chinese New Year?

The Chinese New Year begins on the first full moon between 21 January and 19 February. The celebrations last for two weeks and begin with visits to friends and relatives. On the last day, big street parades are often held.

? DO YOU KNOW

Chinese New Year parades are often headed by a giant dragon. It weaves through the streets to the noise of gongs and firecrackers, to keep away evil spirits.

Who was Santa Claus?

The name Santa Claus comes from Saint Nicholas, a Christian bishop who lived over 1500 years ago. These days the saint is remembered in many countries as Father Christmas or Santa Claus.

Santa Claus is well known as the kindly old gentleman who brings children presents at Christmas.

Why do we wear different clothes?

We wear different clothes for different purposes – such as for work or leisure, or for protection against the weather. Some clothes are worn only on special occasions, and others simply because they are fashionable.

Desert people's robes are ideal for keeping off the hot sun during the day and for providing warmth during the cold nights.

The Amish people in the USA have religious reasons for wearing simple black clothes designed in the style of the 1800s.

Women in Brittany, in France, often wear traditional clothes at festival times. Their tall lace headdresses are called *coiffes*.

18

Some people wear uniforms to show what their job is. This uniform is worn by Canada's Royal Mounted Police.

CLOTHES FACTS

● At £1 million each, the US shuttle astronauts' spacesuits are the most expensive clothes ever made.

● The zip fastener was invented last century, but it took 50 years to produce a version that didn't pop open.

● The most expensive fabric is vicuna, at over £4000 a metre.

In Japan, the kimono first made its appearance over 1000 years ago. It is still sometimes worn by both men and women.

In many countries, everyday dress depends on fashion. The type of clothes that are in fashion changes all the time.

DESIGN A COSTUME

Do you know what your country's national costume looks like? Try designing your own version, basing it on a mixture of old and new styles of clothing.

When were the first theatres built?

No one knows when people first started acting and making up plays, but we do know that the first theatres were built by the Ancient Greeks about 7000 years ago. Greek plays developed from a yearly festival to worship a god called Dionysus. During the celebrations, tales of gods and heroes were told in songs and dances.

DO YOU KNOW

The first Greek plays were called tragedies, from the Greek words for 'goat song'. Goats were sacrificed during the plays.

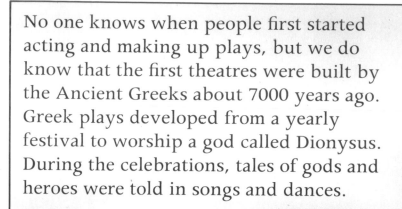

Hardly any objects were used to show where each scene was taking place. The audience relied on the actors to describe the location.

At the back of the theatre was a building called the skene. It was used as a place to change costumes during a performance.

The chorus danced and sang in the circular area called the orchestra. Their role was to comment on the play.

DO YOU KNOW

Kabuki is a spectacular form of Japanese drama. The actors wear colourful costumes and the story is told through a mixture of words, songs and mime. Performances can last over four hours.

The audience sat in rows of seats built into a sloping hillside. The largest theatres could hold up to 17,000 people.

Why do we play music?

Music has always been important to us because it affects our emotions. It can make us feel relaxed or excited, and happy or sad. Even if you can't play a musical instrument, you can still have great fun by singing or dancing to music.

DO YOU KNOW

The earliest music was played to keep gods and spirits happy. Some tribes in remote places still use music for the same reason.

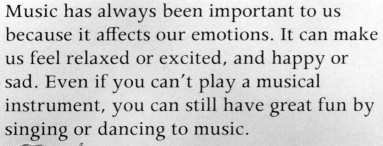

Most modern music relies on electronic instruments such as the electric guitar.

The violin has been one of the most widely used musical instruments for 500 years.

The didgeridoo has been played by Australian Aborigines for thousands of years.

When did painting begin?

The earliest paintings ever found were done 27,000 years ago, on cave walls in France. They show pictures of wild animals such as bison, deer and horses. The painters might have been trying to work magic to improve their hunting.

DO YOU KNOW

The world's most valuable painting is the Mona Lisa by Leonardo da Vinci. It's not for sale, but it's insured for over US $100 million.

Cave dwellers made their paints from plants, berries, earth and pieces of burnt wood. They mixed the materials together to create different colours.

Which is the oldest sport?

The oldest sport of all is wrestling, which goes back at least 4500 years. The sport is still very popular all over the world. In Japan, sumo wrestlers are national heroes and huge crowds go to see their matches.

Sumo wrestlers try to force their opponents to the ground or out of the ring.

When were the first Olympic Games?

The first Olympic Games were held at Olympus in Greece nearly 3000 years ago. After 1000 years, the tradition of holding games every four years died out. It was not revived until 1896 – after a gap of 1500 years.

DO YOU KNOW

Before each Olympics, a special torch is lit at Olympus. It is held in front of a mirror until it is lit by the heat of the Sun. The torch is then carried by runners all the way to the city where the games are being held. The final runner enters the stadium and lights a flame that burns throughout the games.

During the Games, there are usually several events going on at the same time.

Which is the most popular sport?

Soccer is the most popular sport of all. It's played and watched by millions of people everywhere. Many countries have several big soccer clubs, whose teams regularly play against each other. The top players can earn huge sums of money.

● One version of soccer played 700 years ago involved hundreds of players in each team. Games were played between towns, with the goals up to a kilometre apart.

● The longest ever soccer match lasted 3 hours, 30 minutes. It was a drawn cup match held in Brazil.

● The match with the most goals was between two Yugo-slavian teams. The score was 134–1!

The soccer World Cup is held every four years. Over 100 national soccer teams take part in the early rounds.

At the end of the competition the winning team is presented with a magnificent trophy made of solid gold.

Well over a billion people watch the World Cup – in soccer stadiums and on television all round the world.

Brazil and Italy have both won the World Cup three times. Brazil has appeared in every competition since it began in 1930.

23

How many different jobs are there?

There are thousands and thousands of different jobs. In the US, the Department of Labor puts the figure at about 20,000. Some people such as farmers spend most of their time outdoors. Others such as shopkeepers and office staff work indoors. These days, schools often offer advice to help you decide which job you want to do.

 DO YOU KNOW

The first industry began in Ethiopia, 2 million years ago, chipping axe heads and other tools from flint stones.

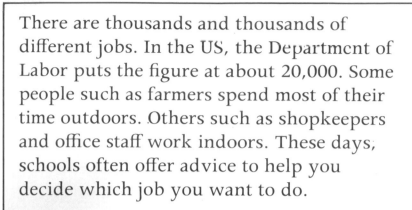

Farming provides many of the basic things we need, such as fruit, vegetables, milk, meat and wool.

Service jobs such as road-sweeping and rubbish collection are important to keep the country running.

 A JOB ALPHABET

How many jobs can you think of? Try making a list of jobs, starting with A for author, and ending with Z for zookeeper. You may have to make some up!

Millions of people work in factories, making goods from tiny electronic devices to huge spacecraft.

Building work employs people from all kinds of trades, such as bricklayers, plumbers and carpenters.

JOB FACTS

● The biggest employer in the world is Indian Railways, with over 1.5 million staff.

● One of the biggest industries is car manufacturing. Every year, 7 million cars are made in Japan alone.

Lawyers and judges train for years before they are fully qualified to work in the legal profession.

Shops of all sizes sell us the goods we need. The biggest stores employ hundreds of people.

In towns and cities, many people spend most of the working day at their desks in office buildings.

What is the most popular food?

Rice is the world's most popular food – more of it is eaten than of any other type of crop. It is mostly grown in Asian countries such as China, Japan and India. There are countless varieties of rice – over 1000 are grown in India alone!

Rice is grown in flooded fields called paddies. In most places it is still picked by hand.

Who eats the most food?

People in wealthy countries eat the most food. North Americans eat the most food per person, followed by Western Europeans.

The energy food gives you is measured in calories. Most adults need about 2300 calories a day but people in poor countries often eat less than 2000.

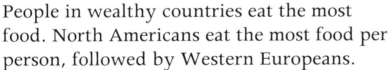

People in wealthy countries eat a wide range of foods. These include a lot of meat and milk products.

In poorer places, people eat fewer milk products and less meat – but more rice, fish and vegetables.

Where are the biggest farms?

The world's biggest farms are in the USSR, North America, Australia and South America. Some cover more than 25,000 hectares – this is over 500 times as big as the Vatican City State. In all, about one third of the world's land area is used for farming. Hundreds of years ago, most people farmed in some way. Today modern farming methods and machines have meant that far fewer farmers are needed.

DO YOU KNOW

Farms that supply beef for burgers are being blamed for the loss of important rainforests in Central America and Brazil. Millions of trees have been cut down to give the cattle somewhere to graze.

Giant farms rely on machines such as combine harvesters. These cut down wheat and separate the grain from the straw.

Wheat has a huge number of uses – it is made into breads, breakfast cereals, macaroni and many other products.

FARMING FACTS

• Farming is thought to have begun about 10,000 years ago in the Middle East, when tribes started breeding animals and growing plants from seeds.

• Some Australian sheep stations have more than 60,000 sheep.

• Silk comes from silkworms raised on special farms. Each silkworm can provide up to 900 metres of silk thread!

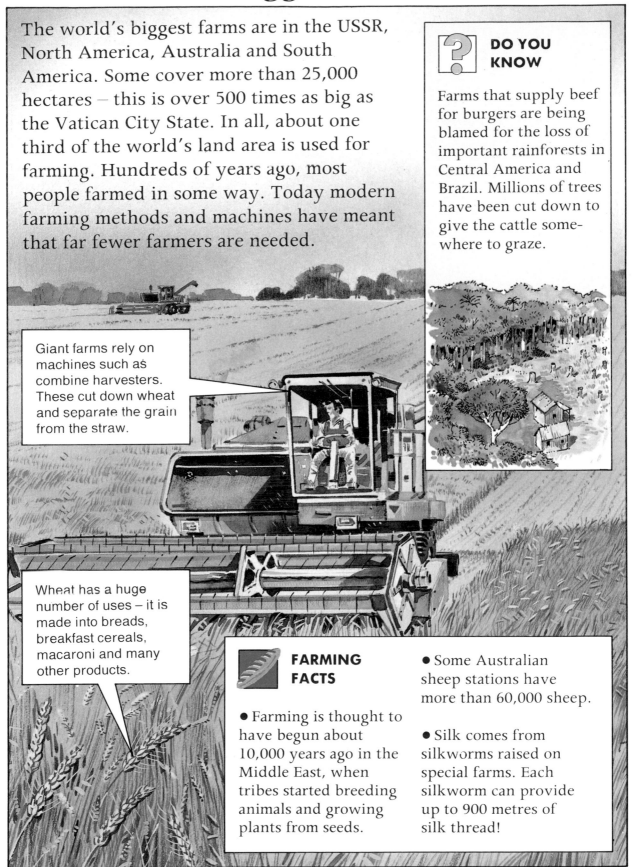

Do all children go to school?

Nowadays, children in most countries have to go to school until they are teenagers. Many are able to continue their studies at colleges and universities. This is quite a recent development. Millions of people alive today have never been to school, and two-thirds of the world's population cannot read or write!

? DO YOU KNOW

The Sumerians and Ancient Egyptians set up the first schools 5000 years ago. Students were taught writing and maths by copying out work over and over again.

In hot places such as India, schoolchildren often have their lessons outside in the fresh air.

Only about a third of children in India stay on to finish their education. Most leave early to start work.

Nowadays, more than eight out of ten young Indian children go to school – far more than a few years ago.

What is the School of the Air?

Children on Australian farms often live a long way from the nearest school. That's why they join the School of the Air. They talk to their teachers by radio and send off their written work by post.

Why do some schools have uniforms?

Some schools think that uniforms help children from different backgrounds feel they all belong to the same group. School uniforms are worn in many countries, but most schools let pupils wear what they like.

What are minerals?

Minerals are materials found in the ground – the word mineral means something that has been mined. There are about 2500 minerals in all, including metals such as gold and silver, and gems, or precious stones, such as diamonds. Minerals have been important to us ever since our earliest ancestors used them to make flint tools.

DO YOU KNOW

The earliest known mine is in Swaziland, Africa. It dates from 41,000 BC and people dug there for a mineral called iron ore. This was probably used for face painting.

Gold mines are the deepest mines in the world. The shaft may go down 2 or 3 kilometres underground.

Rubble is taken from the rock face in trucks. It is then crushed and the gold is carefully separated out.

Workers drill deep holes into the mine walls and place explosives in them to blow the rocks apart.

MINERAL FACTS

● Over half the world's gold is mined in one area of South Africa. The deepest mines are found there, too.

● The most precious gems are diamonds, sapphires and emeralds.

● Cut and polished diamonds only weigh about half as much as when they were found.

● Diamond is the world's hardest natural substance. It is used in industry for drill tips.

● Quartz, found in sand and rock, is the most common mineral.

Which are the main fuels?

The main types of fuel are oil, natural gas and coal. These are all fossil fuels – they were formed millions of years ago from the bodies of animals and plants – and they are all found in deposits deep underground or below the sea bed.

The most important fuel is oil. Without it we'd have no petrol, diesel or paraffin. And that's not all – oil is used for plastics, medicines, perfumes and soaps as well!

In an oil well, long drills cut down to the oil deposits beneath the ocean bed. The oil is then pumped out through pipes.

Oil platforms are often sited far out to sea. Helicopters are the quickest way of bringing in workers and supplies.

Ocean oil wells have huge metal legs anchored to the sea bed. The workers live on the platform high above the waves.

? DO YOU KNOW

The world's supply of fossil fuels will run out in the next 100 years. We'll need new sources of energy to replace them.

Scientists are now experimenting with ways to use natural energy sources that are not going to run out, such as the Sun, the ocean tides and the wind. In some places 'wind farms' have already been set up. These have lots of windmill-like blades which spin round and make electricity.

Why are houses so different?

The types of building used for houses depend on the materials available, the weather, and what purpose the house is to be used for.

House styles vary from area to area. In hot places, for example, houses need to be cool inside, but in cold places they need to be as warm as possible. Some houses in Japan have paper walls to reduce damage in earthquakes, and in some rainy areas houses are built on stilts to avoid flooding.

HOUSE FACTS

● Thousands of people are still living in caves. They are called troglodytes.

● Roman houses built 2000 years ago often had central heating.

● Houses were lit by oil lamps and candles until about 1840.

Very large houses such as French châteaux were built to house dozens of servants as well as the owners of the property.

Many people live in caravans. Old-style horse-drawn gipsy caravans like this one can still be found in parts of Europe.

In hot parts of Africa, mud huts are still common. These have thick mud walls and small windows to help keep out the heat.

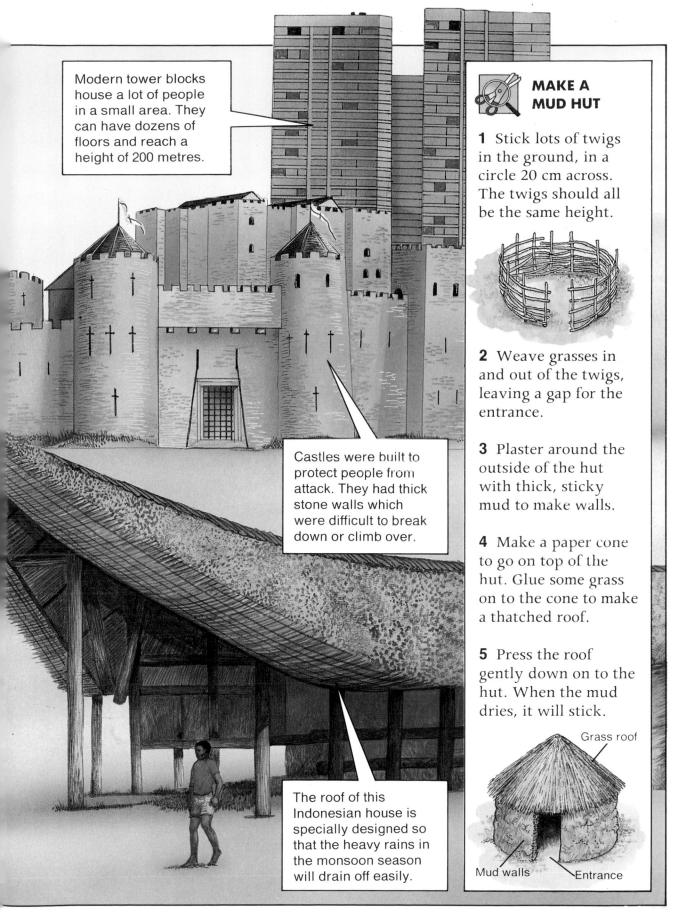

Modern tower blocks house a lot of people in a small area. They can have dozens of floors and reach a height of 200 metres.

Castles were built to protect people from attack. They had thick stone walls which were difficult to break down or climb over.

The roof of this Indonesian house is specially designed so that the heavy rains in the monsoon season will drain off easily.

MAKE A MUD HUT

1 Stick lots of twigs in the ground, in a circle 20 cm across. The twigs should all be the same height.

2 Weave grasses in and out of the twigs, leaving a gap for the entrance.

3 Plaster around the outside of the hut with thick, sticky mud to make walls.

4 Make a paper cone to go on top of the hut. Glue some grass on to the cone to make a thatched roof.

5 Press the roof gently down on to the hut. When the mud dries, it will stick.

Grass roof

Mud walls

Entrance

How do people live in the Sahara Desert?

The people who live in the Sahara Desert are nomads, or wanderers, who travel around in search of places where their camels and goats can graze. They belong to tribes such as the Bedouins, who often live in tents made of animal skins and goat hair.

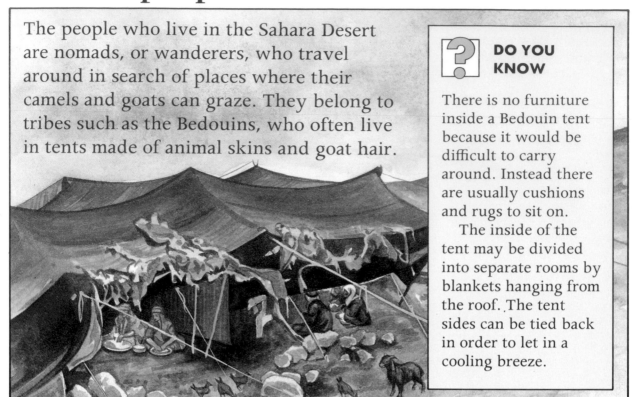

How do people live in the Arctic?

Arctic people such as the Inuit once lived in tents or simple homes made from snow blocks or logs and earth. They got their food and clothing from fishing and hunting. Nowadays, though, things are different – most Inuit live in towns with modern houses and cars.

The traditional Inuit dog-pulled sleds have been largely replaced by skidoos, which have skis on the front to glide over the snow.

How do people live in the Himalayas?

The Himalayas, in Asia, form the highest mountain chain in the world. Many of the people who live in this region are shepherds who move around with their small flocks of yaks, sheep and goats. There are few large buildings other than monasteries.

? DO YOU KNOW

Yaks provide Himalayan people with hair for tents and clothes, and milk to drink. Even their dung is used – as fuel for fires!

The rocky slopes of the Himalayas mean there are few roads. The main means of transport is the yak.

How do people live in the Amazon?

The Amazon is an area of dense rainforest, where it is hot, damp and gloomy. Even so, it is still home to thousands of Amazon Indians who live in villages and spend their time hunting and gathering food.

? DO YOU KNOW

Some Amazon Indians use poison-tipped arrows to hunt forest animals such as monkeys. The poison comes from the tiny arrow-poison frog (below). It is so strong that one scratch from an arrow causes rapid death.

What is a city?

A city is an area where huge numbers of people live and work. There are hundreds of cities in the world, and about 80 of them have populations of over 1 million people. Each country has a capital city, which is usually where the government is based.

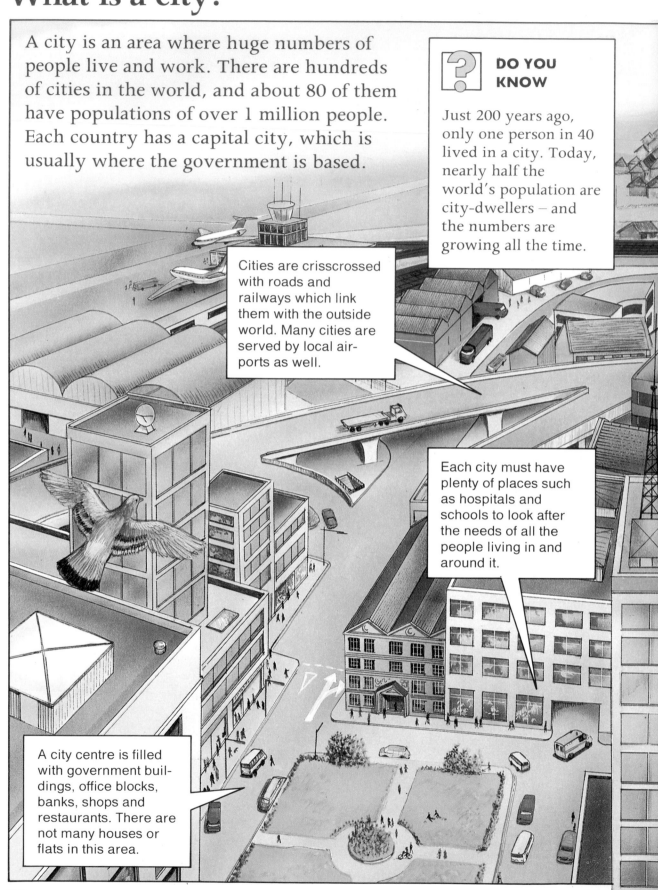

DO YOU KNOW

Just 200 years ago, only one person in 40 lived in a city. Today, nearly half the world's population are city-dwellers – and the numbers are growing all the time.

Cities are crisscrossed with roads and railways which link them with the outside world. Many cities are served by local airports as well.

Each city must have plenty of places such as hospitals and schools to look after the needs of all the people living in and around it.

A city centre is filled with government buildings, office blocks, banks, shops and restaurants. There are not many houses or flats in this area.

Most city-dwellers live away from the centre, in the suburbs. These are recently built areas of housing that have grown up around the edges of a city.

One of the attractions of a city is the number of places where you can go to watch or play sport – such as football stadiums, ice-rinks or swimming pools.

There are usually lots of places for people to visit in their spare time, such as famous buildings, museums, art galleries, theatres and cinemas.

MAKE A CITY PLAN

Some modern cities such as Brasilia in Brazil have been specially thought out by expert planners. Imagine you have been given the job of planning a new city to be built in your area.

You'll need a large piece of paper or card, as well as a pencil and some pens, a ruler and an eraser.

Starting from the city centre, draw in all the things you think would make your city a good place to live in. Don't forget to give it a name.

How will we live in the future?

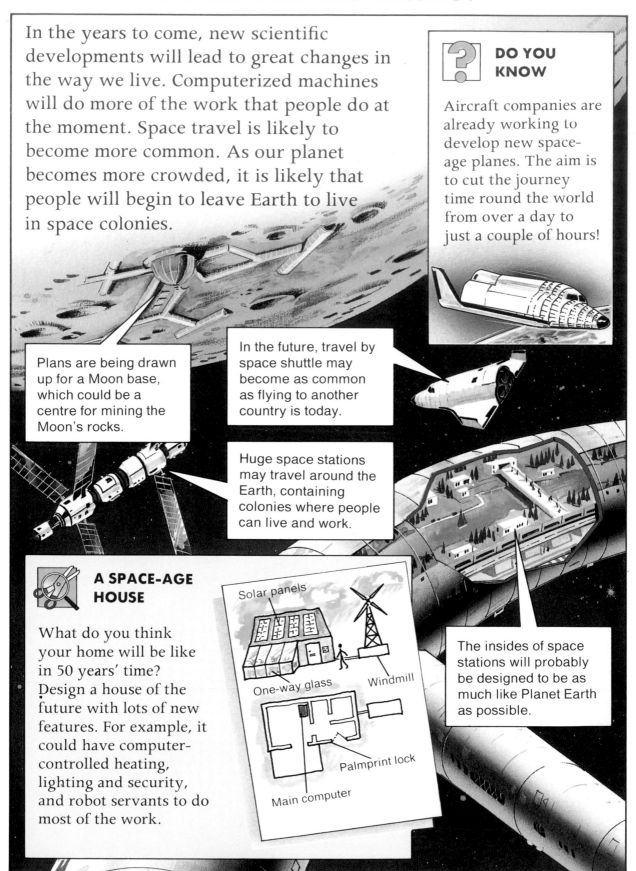

In the years to come, new scientific developments will lead to great changes in the way we live. Computerized machines will do more of the work that people do at the moment. Space travel is likely to become more common. As our planet becomes more crowded, it is likely that people will begin to leave Earth to live in space colonies.

DO YOU KNOW

Aircraft companies are already working to develop new space-age planes. The aim is to cut the journey time round the world from over a day to just a couple of hours!

Plans are being drawn up for a Moon base, which could be a centre for mining the Moon's rocks.

In the future, travel by space shuttle may become as common as flying to another country is today.

Huge space stations may travel around the Earth, containing colonies where people can live and work.

A SPACE-AGE HOUSE

What do you think your home will be like in 50 years' time? Design a house of the future with lots of new features. For example, it could have computer-controlled heating, lighting and security, and robot servants to do most of the work.

Solar panels

One-way glass

Windmill

Palmprint lock

Main computer

The insides of space stations will probably be designed to be as much like Planet Earth as possible.

Useful words

Ancestor   Our ancestors are all the people who lived before us. Our earliest ancestors were the first humans, who inhabited the Earth nearly 2 million years ago.

Climate   Different parts of the world have different weather patterns. Some places are mainly hot and dry, for example, while others are mainly cold and wet. The type of weather an area has is called its climate.

Colony   A group of people who have settled together in a new place.

Drama   The general name for theatrical plays. Tragedy is a type of drama where the stories have a sad ending.

Festival   A celebration of a special event – often with dancing, music and feasting.

Fuel   A substance that can be made to provide heat or energy. Fossil fuels such as oil were formed millions of years ago from the remains of plants and animals. Non-fossil fuels include wood and uranium, which is used in nuclear power stations.

General election   A general election takes place when the people of a nation elect, or choose, their government. This is done by voting – marking a piece of paper to show what your choice is.

Government   The group of people who run a country. There are several forms of government, but the most common is democracy – where a new government is chosen every few years through a general election.

Industry   Work that involves the manufacture, or making, of goods. In factories, production lines pass goods from one stage of manufacturing to the next.

A car production line

Language   The words we use to communicate with each other. Most languages can be written down, using letters or picture symbols.

Monastery   A place where religious men called monks live and work. Monasteries are often to be found in remote places such as high up in the mountains.

Nomads   People who wander from place to place and have no fixed home, such as desert tribes and some gipsies.

Tourist   The general word for a person who is on holiday away from home. The word tourist was originally used for someone who was on a tour.

Index

A
Abraham 15
Africa 4, 10, 30, 32
Amazon 35
ancestor 4, 39
Ancient Egyptians 28
Ancient Greeks 20
Arabic 10
Arctic 34
Asia 4
Australia 27, 29
Austria 9

B
Bedouins 34
Brazil 23, 27, 37
Buddhism 15
burgers 27

C
calories 26
Canada 9, 19
capital city 36, 37
Central America 27
China 4, 11, 26
Chinese New Year 17
Christianity 14, 15
cities 25, 36–37
climate 8, 39
clothes 18–19
coal 31, 39
colony 38, 39
communist 12
country 6, 8, 12

D
Damascus 37
democracy 12, 39
Denmark 7
dependencies 7
dictator 12
drama 20, 39

E
Egypt 10
energy 26, 39
English 11
Ethiopia 24

F
factories 24, 39
farm 24, 27, 29
fashion 18, 19
festival 16, 20, 39
flag 6
flint tools 24, 30
food 26

fossil fuels 31, 39
France 9, 18
fuel 31, 39

G
gems 30
general election 12, 39
Germany 29
gipsies 29, 32
gold 30
government 6, 12, 13, 36, 39
Greece 23
Greenland 7

H
hieroglyphs 10
Himalayas 35
Hindi 10
Hinduism 14
houses 32–33, 36, 37, 38

I
independent country 6, 8
India 10, 14, 15, 25, 26, 28
Indonesia 33
industry 24, 25, 30, 39
Inuit 34
Islam 14, 15
Italy 8, 9, 23

J
Japan 4, 10, 19, 20, 22, 25
Japanese language 10
Jesus Christ 5, 14
jobs 24–25
Judaism 15

L
language 10–11, 39
laws 6, 12

M
Mandarin 11
Mardi Gras 16
metals 30
Middle East 10, 27
minerals 30
monastery 35, 39
Muhammad 15
music 21

N
nation 6, 39
national anthem 6
national costume 19
natural gas 31
Netherlands 29

nomads 34, 39
North America 27

O
oil 31, 39
Olympic Games 23

P
painting 21
parliament 13
passport 9
population 4, 8, 15, 28, 36

R
rainforest 27, 35
religions 14–15
Roman Catholic Church 8
Rome 8

S
Sahara Desert 34
Santa Claus 19
school uniforms 29
schools 24, 28–29, 36
Siddharta Gautama 15
soccer 23
South America 10, 27
space travel 38
Spain 9, 10
Spanish 10
sport 22–23, 37
Sumerians 28
Swahili 10
Syria 37

T
taxes 12, 13
theatres 20
tourist 9, 39
tragedy 20, 39
tribes 21, 27, 34

U
UK 9, 13
United Kingdom 13
United Nations 12
USA 9, 18, 24
USSR 8, 27

V
Vatican City State 8, 27
voting 12, 39

W
wheat 27
World Cup 23
wrestling 22